I Love Color!
Quilt Collection

LEISURE ARTS, INC.
Little Rock, Arkansas

EDITORIAL STAFF
Vice President of Editorial: Susan White Sullivan
Special Projects Director: Susan Frantz Wiles
Director of E-Commerce and Prepress Services: Mark Hawkins
Creative Art Director: Katherine Laughlin
Art Publications Director: Rhonda Shelby
Technical Editor: Lisa Lancaster
Technical Writer: Frances Huddleston
Associate Technical Writer: Jean Lewis
Editorial Writer: Susan McManus Johnson
Art Category Manager: Lora Puls
Graphic Artists: Stacy Owens and Becca Snider Tally
Imaging Technician: Stephanie Johnson
Prepress Technician: Janie Marie Wright
Contributing Photographer: Ken West
Contributing Photo Stylist: Sondra Daniel
Manager of E-Commerce: Robert Young

BUSINESS STAFF
President and Chief Executive Officer: Rick Barton
Vice President of Finance: Laticia Mull Dittrich
Director of Corporate Planning: Anne Martin
National Sales Director: Martha Adams
Information Technology Director: Brian Roden
Controller: Francis Caple
Vice President of Operations: Jim Dittrich
Retail Customer Service Manager: Stan Raynor
Vice President of Purchasing: Fred F. Pruss

Library of Congress Control Number: 2012946883

ISBN-13: 978-1-4647-0253-2

4

32

18

26

38

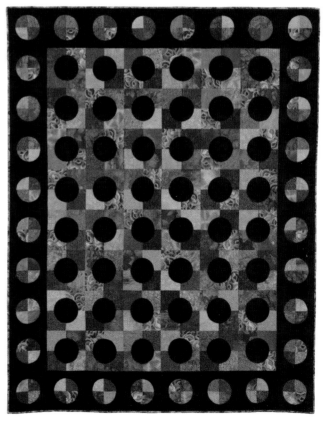

46

MELON SLICES

Finished Throw Quilt Size: 53" x 65"
(135 cm x 165 cm)
Finished Block Size: Approximately 8$^1/_2$" x 8$^1/_2$"
(22 cm x 22 cm)

WHAT YOU WILL NEED

*Yardage is based on 43"/44" (109 cm/112 cm) wide fabric
with a usable width of 40" (102 cm).*

2 yds (1.8 m) of blue large floral fabric
$^5/_8$ yd (57 cm) of blue small floral fabric
$^1/_2$ yd (46 cm) *total* of assorted blue print fabrics
$^1/_4$ yd (23 cm) of orange dot fabric
1$^3/_4$ yds (1.6 m) *total* of assorted orange print fabrics
1$^5/_8$ yds (1.5 m) of white dot fabric
4$^1/_8$ yds (3.8 m) of fabric for backing
$^7/_8$ yd (80 cm) of fabric for binding
61" x 73" (155 cm x 185 cm) piece of batting
4$^1/_2$ yds (4.1 m) of 18" (46 cm) wide lightweight
  fusible interfacing
Template plastic
Stabilizer
Black fine-point permanent felt-tip pen
Removable fabric marking pen
Point turning tool
Clear monofilament thread *(optional)*

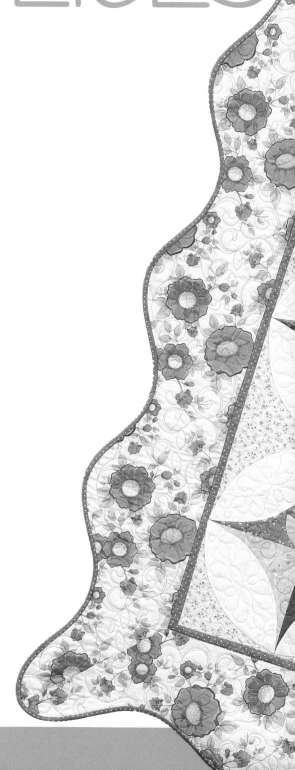

CUTTING THE PIECES

*Follow **Rotary Cutting**, page 53, to cut fabric. Cut all strips from the selvage-to-selvage width of the fabric unless otherwise indicated. Outer borders are cut longer than needed and will be trimmed to fit quilt top center. All measurements include $^1/_4$" seam allowances.*

From blue large floral fabric:
- Cut 2 *lengthwise* **side outer borders** 8" x $68^1/_2$".
- Cut 2 *lengthwise* **top/bottom outer borders** 8" x $56^1/_2$".

From blue small floral fabric:
- Cut 1 strip $13^1/_4$" wide. From this strip, cut 3 squares $13^1/_4$" x $13^1/_4$". Cut squares *twice* diagonally to make 12 **side setting triangles**. (You will use 10 and have 2 left over.)
- Cut 1 strip $6^7/_8$" wide. From this strip, cut 2 squares $6^7/_8$" x $6^7/_8$". Cut squares *once* diagonally to make 4 **corner setting triangles**.

From assorted blue print fabrics:
- Cut 72 **small rectangles** 2" x $3^1/_2$".

From orange dot fabric:
- Cut 5 **inner border strips** 1" wide.

From assorted orange print fabrics:
- Cut 36 squares $6^7/_8$" x $6^7/_8$". Cut squares *once* diagonally to make 72 **triangles**.

From white dot fabric:
- Cut 12 strips $4^1/_4$" wide. From these strips, cut 48 **large rectangles** $4^1/_4$" x $9^1/_2$".

From fabric for binding:
- Cut 1 **square for binding** 26" x 26".

From lightweight fusible interfacing:
- Cut 12 strips $9^1/_2$" wide. From these strips, cut 48 **large rectangles** $9^1/_2$" x $4^1/_4$".
- Cut 15 strips 2" wide. From these strips, cut 72 **small rectangles** 2" x $3^1/_2$".

MAKING THE MELON SLICES

1. To make templates, place template plastic over patterns, page 17. Trace patterns with permanent pen. Carefully cut patterns out along drawn lines.
2. Center **small melon slice template** on non-fusible side of fusible interfacing **small rectangle** (**Fig. 1**). Trace around template with pencil; remove template.

Fig. 1

3. Place marked interfacing **small rectangle**, fusible side down, on right side of 1 blue print **small rectangle**; *do not iron* rectangles. Stitch along traced lines. Trim excess fabric and interfacing approximately $^1/_4$" outside stitching line; trim points. Cut a slit in center of interfacing, making sure not to cut blue fabric (**Fig. 2**).

Fig. 2

4. Turn small melon slice right side out. ***Do not iron*** melon slice. Insert point turning tool through slit and gently push while finger pressing along seam to crease a smooth edge.

Small Melon Slice

5. Repeat Steps 2-4 to make 72 **small melon slices**.
6. In the same manner, use interfacing **large rectangles**, white dot **large rectangles**, and **large melon slice template** to make 48 **large melon slices**.

Large Melon Slice (make 48)

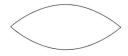

MAKING THE BLOCKS

Follow **Piecing**, *page 54, and* **Pressing**, *page 55, to make quilt top. Use ¹/₄" seam allowances throughout.*

1. Sew 2 orange print **triangles** together to make to make **Unit 1**. Make 36 Unit 1's.

Unit 1 (make 36)

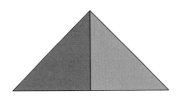

2. Sew 2 **Unit 1's** together to make **Unit 2**. Make 18 Unit 2's.

Unit 2 (make 18)

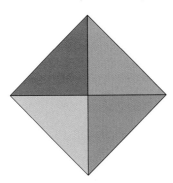

3. Arrange 4 **small melon slices** in center of 1 **Unit 2** and fuse. Following **Machine Appliqué**, page 56, and using clear monofilament or matching thread, stitch around edges of small melon slices to make **Block**. Make 18 Blocks.

Block (make 18)

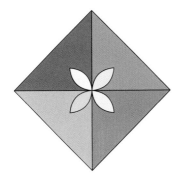

ASSEMBLING THE QUILT TOP

1. Referring to **Assembly Diagram**, sew **Blocks**, **side setting triangles**, and **corner setting triangles** into *diagonal* Rows.
2. Sew **Rows** together to make quilt top center.
3. Referring to **Quilt Top Diagram**, page 9, and leaving ¹/₄" seam allowances around outer edge of quilt top, arrange **large melon slices** on quilt top center; fuse. In the same manner as small melon slices, appliqué large melon slices to quilt top center.

Assembly Diagram

7

4. Using diagonal seams (**Fig. 3**), sew **inner border strips** together, end to end, to make 1 continuous strip.

Fig. 3

5. Follow **Adding Squared Borders**, page 57, to add **side**, then **top** and **bottom inner borders**.
6. Follow **Adding Mitered Borders**, page 57, to add **outer borders**.

COMPLETING THE QUILT

1. Follow **Quilting**, page 58, to mark, layer, and quilt as desired. Quilt shown is machine quilted. A curlicue pattern is quilted in the orange areas around the small melon slices, and a feather motif is quilted in each large melon slice. The setting triangles are quilted with a continuous loop pattern. The inner border is quilted in the ditch. The outer border is quilted with a continuous vine pattern.

2. Referring to **Fig. 4**, use removable fabric marking pen to mark inner and outer points of scallops (shown in purple). Draw a curving line through marks (shown in pink). Stay stitch approximately ¹/₈" inside drawn line. Cut along drawn line through all layers.

Fig. 4

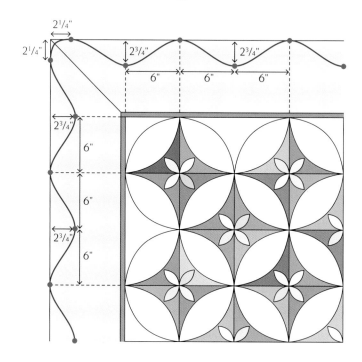

3. Use **square for binding** and follow **Making a Continuous Bias Strip**, page 61, to make 2¹/₄" bias binding.
4. Matching wrong sides and raw edges, carefully press bias binding in half lengthwise.
5. Press one end of binding diagonally (**Fig. 5**).

Fig. 5

6. Beginning with pressed end of binding (folded triangle shape facing up), match raw edges of binding to raw edge of quilt top. Use a $^1/_4$" seam allowance to sew binding to quilt. When sewing around scallops, pin binding to one scallop at a time. Gently ease binding around curves, being careful not to stretch it.

7. Continue sewing binding to quilt until binding overlaps beginning end by approximately 2". Trim excess binding.

8. Fold binding over to quilt backing and pin pressed edge in place covering stitching line.

9. Blindstitch (page 64) binding to backing, taking care not to stitch through to front of quilt.

Quilted by Laurie Vandergriff of Spring Creek Quilting.

Quilt Top Diagram

(Continued on page 12.)

	TWIN
Finished Size	65" x 89" (165 cm x 226 cm)
Blocks	39
What You Will Need	$2^5/_8$ yds (2.4 m) of blue large floral fabric $^7/_8$ yd (80 cm) of blue small floral fabric 1 yd (91 cm) *total* of assorted blue print fabrics $^1/_4$ yd (23 cm) of orange dot fabric $3^3/_8$ yds (3.1 m) *total* of assorted orange print fabrics $3^1/_8$ yds (2.9 m) of white dot fabric $5^1/_2$ yds (5 m) of fabric for backing 1 yd (91 cm) of fabric for binding 73" x 97" (185 cm x 246 cm) piece of batting 9 yds (8.2 m) of 18" (46 cm) wide lightweight fusible interfacing Template plastic Stabilizer Black fine-point permanent felt-tip pen Removable fabric marking pen Point turning tool Clear monofilament thread *(optional)*
Cut Pieces	2 *lengthwise* blue large floral **side outer borders** 8" x $92^1/_2$" 2 *lengthwise* blue large floral **top/bottom outer borders** 8" x $68^1/_2$" 4 blue small floral squares $13^1/_4$" x $13^1/_4$" cut *twice* diagonally to make 16 **side setting triangles** 2 blue small floral squares $6^7/_8$" x $6^7/_8$" cut *once* diagonally to make 4 **corner setting triangles** 156 assorted blue print **small rectangles** 2" x $3^1/_2$" 7 orange dot **inner border strips** 1" wide 78 assorted orange print squares $6^7/_8$" x $6^7/_8$" cut *once* diagonally to make 156 **triangles** 96 white dot **large rectangles** $4^1/_4$" x $9^1/_2$" 1 **square for binding** 30" x 30" 96 fusible web **large rectangles** $9^1/_2$" x $4^1/_4$" 156 fusible web **small rectangles** 2" x $3^1/_2$"

Twin Size Quilt Top Diagram

	QUEEN
Finished Size	89" x 101" (226 cm x 257 cm)
Blocks	72
What You Will Need	3 yds (2.7 m) of blue large floral fabric 1^1/$_8$ yds (1 m) of blue small floral fabric 1^3/$_4$ yds (1.6 m) *total* of assorted blue print fabrics ^{3}/$_8$ yds (34 cm) of orange dot fabric 6^1/$_8$ yds (5.6 m) *total* of assorted orange print fabrics 5^1/$_2$ yds (5 m) of white dot fabric 8^1/$_8$ yds (7.4 m) of fabric for backing 1^1/$_8$ yds (1 m) of fabric for binding 97" x 109" (246 cm x 277 cm) piece of batting 15^3/$_4$ yds (14.4 m) of 18" (46 cm) wide lightweight fusible interfacing Template plastic Stabilizer Black fine-point permanent felt-tip pen Removable fabric marking pen Point turning tool Clear monofilament thread *(optional)*
Cut Pieces	2 *lengthwise* blue large floral **side outer borders** 8" x 104^1/$_2$" 2 *lengthwise* blue large floral **top/bottom outer borders** 8" x 92^1/$_2$" 6 blue small floral squares 13^1/$_4$" x 13^1/$_4$" cut *twice* diagonally to make 24 **side setting triangles** (you will use 22, and have 2 left over) 2 blue small floral squares 6^7/$_8$" x 6^7/$_8$" cut *once* diagonally to make 4 **corner setting triangles** 288 assorted blue print **small rectangles** 2" x 3^1/$_2$" 9 orange dot **inner border strips** 1" wide 144 assorted orange print squares 6^7/$_8$" x 6^7/$_8$" cut *once* diagonally to make 288 **triangles** 168 white dot **large rectangles** 4^1/$_4$" x 9^1/$_2$" 1 **square for binding** 33" x 33" 168 fusible web **large rectangles** 9^1/$_2$" x 4^1/$_4$" 288 fusible web **small rectangles** 2" x 3^1/$_2$"

Queen Size Quilt Top Diagram

MELON SLICES
TABLE RUNNER

Finished Table Runner Size: 22^1/$_2$" x 46^1/$_2$"
(57 cm x 118 cm)
Finished Block Size: Approximately 8^1/$_2$" x 8^1/$_2$"
(22 cm x 22 cm)

WHAT YOU WILL NEED

Yardage is based on 43"/44" (109 cm/112 cm) wide fabric with a usable width of 40" (102 cm).

- 1^1/$_2$ yds (1.4 m) of blue large floral fabric
- ^{1}/$_2$ yd (46 cm) of blue small floral fabric
- Scraps of 12 assorted blue print fabrics (each scrap should be at least 2" x 3^1/$_2$")
- ^{1}/$_8$ yd (11 cm) of orange dot fabric
- Scraps of 12 assorted orange print fabrics (each scrap should be at least 7" x 7")
- ^{1}/$_2$ yd (46 cm) of white dot fabric
- 1^1/$_2$ yds (1.4 m) of fabric for backing
- ^{5}/$_8$ yd (57 cm) of fabric for binding
- 26" x 50" (66 cm x 127 cm) piece of batting
- 1^1/$_8$ yds (1 m) of 18" (46 cm) wide lightweight fusible interfacing
- Template plastic
- Stabilizer
- Black fine-point permanent felt-tip pen
- Removable fabric marking pen
- Point turning tool
- Clear monofilament thread *(optional)*

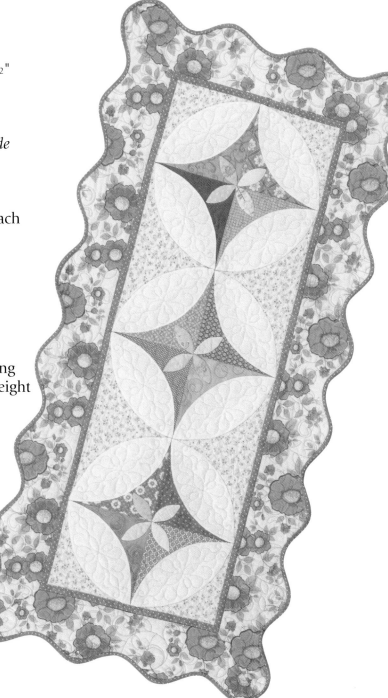

CUTTING THE PIECES

*Follow **Rotary Cutting**, page 53, to cut fabric. Cut all strips from the selvage-to-selvage width unless otherwise indicated. Outer borders are cut longer than needed and will be trimmed to fit table runner top center. All measurements include 1/4" seam allowances.*

From blue large floral fabric:
- Cut 2 *lengthwise* long outer borders 4³/₄" x 50".
- Cut 2 *lengthwise* short outer borders 4³/₄" x 25".

From blue small floral fabric:
- Cut 1 square 13¹/₄" x 13¹/₄". Cut squares *twice* diagonally to make 4 **side setting triangles**.
- Cut 2 squares 6⁷/₈" x 6⁷/₈". Cut squares *once* diagonally to make 4 **corner setting triangles**.

From assorted blue print fabrics:
- Cut 12 **small rectangles** 2" x 3¹/₂".

From orange dot fabric:
- Cut 3 **inner border strips** 1" wide.

From assorted orange print fabrics:
- Cut 12 squares 6⁷/₈" x 6⁷/₈". Cut squares *once* diagonally to make 24 **triangles**. (You will use 12 triangles, 1 from each fabric.)

From white dot fabric:
- Cut 3 strips 4¹/₂" wide. From these strips, cut 12 **large rectangles** 4¹/₂" x 9¹/₂".

From fabric for binding:
- Cut 1 **square for binding** 20" x 20".

From lightweight fusible interfacing:
- Cut 3 strips 9¹/₂" wide. From these strips, cut 12 **large rectangles** 9¹/₂" x 4¹/₂".
- Cut 3 strips 2" wide. From these strips, cut 12 **small rectangles** 2" x 3¹/₂".

MAKING THE TABLE RUNNER TOP

1. Follow **Making the Melon Slices**, page 6, to make 12 **small melon slices** and 12 **large melon slices**.
2. Follow **Making the Blocks**, page 7, to make 3 **Blocks**.
3. Referring to **Assembly Diagram**, sew **Blocks**, **side setting triangles**, and **corner setting triangles** into *diagonal* Rows.
4. Sew **Rows** together to make table runner top center.
5. Referring to **Table Runner Top Diagram**, page 17, and leaving 1/4" seam allowances around outer edge of table runner top center, arrange **large melon slices** on table runner top center; fuse. In the same manner as small melon slices, appliqué **large melon slices** to table runner top center.

Assembly Diagram

6. Using diagonal seams (**Fig. 1**), sew **inner border strips** together, end to end, to make 1 continuous strip.

Fig. 1

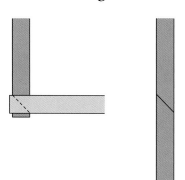

7. Follow **Adding Squared Borders**, page 57, to add **side**, then **top** and **bottom inner borders**.
8. Follow **Adding Mitered Borders**, page 57, to add **outer borders**.

COMPLETING THE TABLE RUNNER

1. Follow **Completing the Quilt**, page 8, to complete table runner with this exception: refer to **Fig. 2** below to scallop edges.

Fig. 2

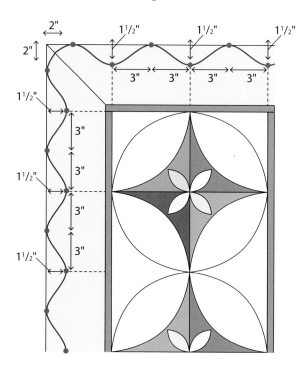

Quilted by Laurie Vandergriff of Spring Creek Quilting.

Table Runner Top Diagram

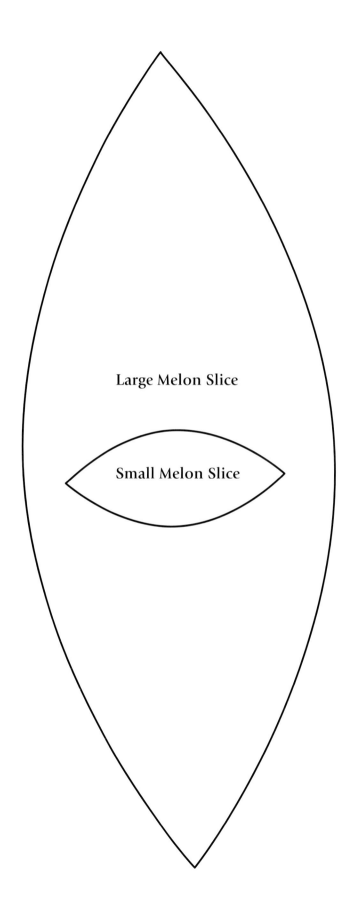

Large Melon Slice

Small Melon Slice

PERENNIAL PINWHEELS

Finished Quilt Size: 79" x 97" (201 cm x 246 cm)
Finished Block Size: 12" x 12" (30 cm x 30 cm)

WHAT YOU WILL NEED

Yardage is based on 43"/44" (109 cm/112 cm) wide fabric with a usable width of 40" (102 cm). Fat quarters are approximately 22" x 18" (56 cm x 46 cm).

- $6^1/_8$ yds (5.6 m) of cream tone-on-tone fabric for blocks
- $1/_4$ yd (23 cm) *each* of 15 assorted dark print fabrics (blues, greens, and purples) for blocks
- 8 fat quarters of assorted bright print fabrics for pinwheels and flanges
- $1/_4$ yd (23 cm) of green print fabric for leaves
- $7^1/_4$ yds (6.6 m) of fabric for backing
- $3/_4$ yd (69 cm) of fabric for binding
- 87" x 105" (221 cm x 267 cm) piece of batting
- 7 yds (6.4 m) of green Clover Quick Bias $1/_4$" (6 mm) wide fusible bias tape for stems

CUTTING THE PIECES

*Follow **Rotary Cutting**, page 53, to cut fabric. Cut all strips from the selvage-to-selvage width of the fabric. Cut strips from fat quarters parallel to the long edge. All measurements include $1/4$" seam allowances.*

From cream tone-on-tone fabric:
- Cut 9 strips 3" wide. From these strips, cut 106 **large squares** 3" x 3".
- Cut 3 strips 2" wide. From these strips, cut 48 **small squares** 2" x 2".
- Cut 46 strips $1^1/2$" wide. From these strips, cut 64 **large rectangles** $1^1/2$" x $8^1/2$", 128 **medium rectangles** $1^1/2$" x $6^1/2$", and 64 **small rectangles** $1^1/2$" x $4^1/2$".
- Cut 3 strips $4^1/2$" wide. From these strips, cut 21 **background squares** $4^1/2$" x $4^1/2$".
- Cut 16 strips $3^1/2$" wide. From these strips, cut 48 **large background rectangles** $3^1/2$" x $10^1/2$".
- Cut 4 strips $2^1/2$" wide. From these strips, cut 24 **medium background rectangles** $2^1/2$" x $5^1/2$".
- Cut 3 strips $2^1/2$" wide. From these strips, cut 21 **small background rectangles** $2^1/2$" x $4^1/2$".
- Cut 5 strips $1^1/2$" wide. From these strips, cut 72 **very small background rectangles** $1^1/2$" x $2^1/2$".

From *each* assorted dark print fabric:
- Cut 3 **strips** $2^1/2$" wide.

From *each* bright print fat quarter:
- Cut 2 strips 3" wide. From these strips, cut 14 **large squares** 3" x 3". (You will use 106 and have 6 left over.)
- Cut 1 strip $6^1/2$" wide. From this strip, cut 16 **flange strips** $7/8$" x $6^1/2$".

From green print fabric:
- Cut 3 strips 2" wide. From these strips, cut 48 **small squares** 2" x 2".

From fabric for binding:
- Cut 10 **binding strips** $2^1/4$" wide.

MAKING THE UNITS FROM STRIP SETS

*Follow **Piecing**, page 54, and **Pressing**, page 55, to make quilt top. Use $1/4$" seam allowances throughout unless otherwise indicated.*

1. Sew 4 **strips** together to make **Strip Set A**. Make 4 Strip Set A's. Cut across Strip Set A's at $2^1/2$" intervals to make 64 **Unit 1's**.

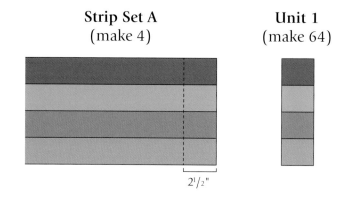

Strip Set A
(make 4)

Unit 1
(make 64)

$2^1/2$"

2. Sew 5 **strips** together to make **Strip Set B**. Cut across Strip Set B at $2^1/2$" intervals to make 6 **Unit 2's**.

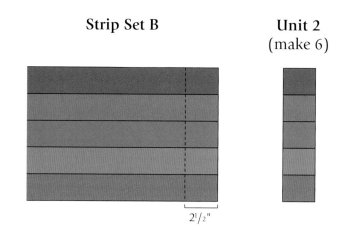

Strip Set B

Unit 2
(make 6)

$2^1/2$"

3. Sew 6 **strips** together to make **Strip Set C**. Make 4 Strip Set C's. Cut across Strip Set C's at 2¹/₂" intervals to make 64 **Unit 3's**.

Strip Set C
(make 4)

Unit 3
(make 64)

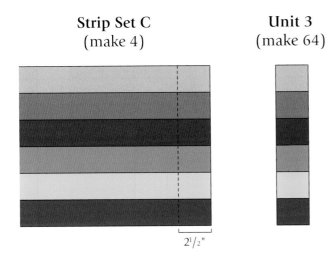

2¹/₂"

MAKING THE PINWHEELS

1. Draw a diagonal line on wrong side of each cream **large square**.
2. For 1 Pinwheel, select 2 matching bright **large squares** and 2 cream **large squares**.
3. Matching right sides, place 1 cream large square on top of 1 bright large square. Stitch ¹/₄" from each side of drawn line (**Fig. 1**). Cut along drawn line and press seam allowances to bright fabric to make 2 **Triangle-Squares**. Make 4 Triangle-Squares. Trim each Triangle-Square to 2¹/₂" x 2¹/₂".

Fig. 1

Triangle-Square (make 4 matching)

4. Sew 4 Triangle-Squares together to make **Pinwheel**. Pinwheel should measure 4¹/₂" x 4¹/₂" including seam allowances.

Pinwheel

5. Repeat Steps 2-4 to make a total of 53 Pinwheels.

MAKING THE BLOCKS

1. Sew 1 **Pinwheel** and 2 **small rectangles** together to make **Unit 4**.

Unit 4

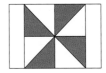

2. Sew **Unit 4** and 2 **medium rectangles** together to make **Unit 5**.

Unit 5

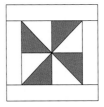

3. For flange, select 4 matching **flange strips** which contrast with the Pinwheel in Unit 5. Matching *wrong* sides and long edges, press flange strips in half.

4. Matching raw edges and using a $1/8$" seam allowance, baste **flange strips** to sides of **Unit 5** (**Fig. 2**). Repeat to baste flange strips to top and bottom edges of Unit 5 (**Fig. 3**).

Fig. 2

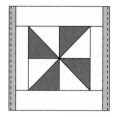

Fig. 3

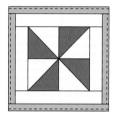

5. Sew **Unit 5** and 2 **medium rectangles** together to make **Unit 6**.

Unit 6

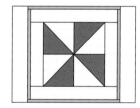

6. Sew **Unit 6** and 2 **large rectangles** together to make **Unit 7**. Unit 7 should measure $8^1/2$" x $8^1/2$" including seam allowances.

Unit 7

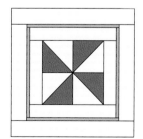

7. Sew **Unit 7** and 2 **Unit 1's** together to make **Unit 8**.

Unit 8

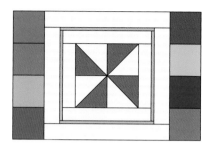

8. Sew **Unit 8** and 2 **Unit 3's** together to make **Block**. Block should measure $12^1/2$" x $12^1/2$" including seam allowances.

Block

9. Repeat Steps 1-8 to make a total of 32 Blocks.

MAKING THE FLOWER AND LEAF UNITS

1. Sew 1 **Pinwheel**, 1 **background square**, and 1 **small background rectangle** together to make **Flower Unit**. Unit should measure 10¹/₂" x 4¹/₂" including seam allowances. Make 21 Flower Units.

Flower Unit (make 21)

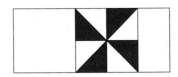

2. Draw a diagonal line on wrong side of each cream **small square**.

3. Matching right sides, place 1 cream small square on top of 1 green small square. Stitch ¹/₄" from each side of drawn line (**Fig. 4**). Cut along drawn line and press seam allowances to green fabric to make 2 **Triangle-Squares**. Make 96 Triangle-Squares. Trim each Triangle-Square to 1¹/₂" x 1¹/₂".

Fig. 4

Triangle-Square (make 96)

4. Sew 2 **Triangle-Squares** together to make **Unit 9a**. Sew 2 **Triangle-Squares** together to make **Unit 9b**. Make 24 Unit 9a's and 24 Unit 9b's.

Unit 9a
(make 24)

Unit 9b
(make 24)

5. Sew 1 **Unit 9a** and 1 **very small background rectangle** together to make **Unit 10a**. Sew 1 **Unit 9b** and 1 **very small background rectangle** together to make **Unit 10b**. Units should measure 2¹/₂" x 2¹/₂" including seam allowances. Make 24 Unit 10a's and 24 Unit 10b's.

Unit 10a
(make 24)

Unit 10b
(make 24)

6. Sew 1 **Unit 10a** and 1 **Unit 10b** together to make **Unit 11**. Make 24 Unit 11's.

Unit 11 (make 24)

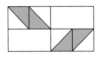

7. Sew 1 **Unit 11**, 1 **medium background rectangle**, and 1 **very small background rectangle** together to make **Unit 12a**. Sew 1 **Unit 11**, 1 **medium background rectangle**, and 1 **very small background rectangle** together to make **Unit 12b**. Units should measure 10¹/₂" x 2¹/₂" including seam allowances. Make 12 Unit 12a's and 12 Unit 12b's.

Unit 12a (make 12)   **Unit 12b** (make 12)

8. Sew 1 **Unit 12a** and 2 **large background rectangles** together to make **Leaf Unit A**. Sew 1 **Unit 12b** and 2 **large background rectangles** together to make **Leaf Unit B**. Leaf Units should measure 10^1/$_2$" x 8^1/$_2$" including seam allowances. Make 12 Leaf Unit A's and 12 Leaf Unit B's.

Leaf Unit A (make 12)

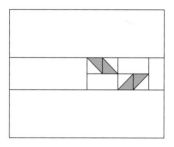

Leaf Unit B (make 12)

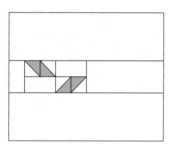

ASSEMBLING THE QUILT TOP
*Refer to **Quilt Top Diagram** to assemble quilt top.*

1. Rotating Blocks as desired, sew 8 **Blocks** together to make *vertical* **Row**. Row should measure 12^1/$_2$" x 96^1/$_2$" including seam allowances. Make 4 Rows.

2. Rotating Flower Units as shown, sew 2 **Unit 2's**, 7 **Flower Units**, 4 **Leaf Unit A's**, and 4 **Leaf Unit B's** together to make **Flower Panel**. Flower Panel should measure 10^1/$_2$" x 96^1/$_2$" including seam allowances. Make 3 Flower Panels.

3. For **vines**, arrange fusible bias tape, cutting lengths as needed, on Flower Panels; pin if desired. At each spot where the vine appears to weave behind a flower, remove stitching and insert end of tape; re-stitch seam. Fuse bias tape in place. Topstitch along edges of vines with matching thread.

4. Sew **Rows** and **Flower Panels** together to complete quilt top.

COMPLETING THE QUILT
1. Stay-stitch around the quilt top approximately ^{1}/$_8$" from edge.

2. Follow **Quilting**, page 58, to mark, layer, and quilt as desired. Quilt shown is machine quilted. A swirling pattern and scalloped border are quilted in each pinwheel block. The cream rectangles of the blocks are quilted in the ditch and the dark squares of the blocks are quilted with a leaf pattern. A butterfly and leaf pattern is quilted in the background of the Flower Panels.

3. Follow **Making a Hanging Sleeve**, page 61, if a hanging sleeve is desired.

4. Use **binding strips** and follow **Making Straight Grain Binding**, page 62, to make binding. Follow **Attaching Binding with Mitered Corners**, page 62, to bind quilt.

Quilted by Laurie Vandergriff of Spring Creek Quilting.

SITKA ROSE

Finished Quilt Size: 60" x 70$^1/_2$" (152 cm x 179 cm)
Finished Block Size: 10$^1/_2$" x 10$^1/_2$" (27 cm x 27 cm)

WHAT YOU WILL NEED
Yardage is based on 43"/44" (109 cm/112 cm) wide fabric with a usable width of 40" (102 cm). Fat quarters are approximately 22" x 18" (56 cm x 46 cm).

   6 fat quarters of assorted green print fabric for blocks
      and leaves
   6 fat quarters of assorted pink print fabric for blocks
      and flowers
   1 fat quarter of tan tone-on-tone fabric for flower centers
   $^7/_8$ yd (80 cm) of dark green tone-on-tone fabric for
      vines
   2$^5/_8$ yds (2.4 m) of cream tone-on-tone fabric for blocks
      and border
   $^7/_8$ yd (80 cm) of multi-color light print fabric for blocks
   4$^3/_8$ yds (4 m) of fabric for backing
   $^5/_8$ yd (57 cm) of fabric for binding
   68" x 78" (173 cm x 198 cm) piece of batting
   Template plastic
   Black fine-point permanent felt-tip pen
   $^1/_4$" (6 mm) bias pressing bar *(optional)*

CUTTING THE PIECES

*Follow **Rotary Cutting**, page 53, to cut fabric. Cut all strips from the selvage-to-selvage width of the fabric. Cut strips from fat quarters parallel to the long edge. Borders are cut longer than needed and will be trimmed to fit quilt top center. All measurements include $^1/_4$" seam allowances.*

From *each* assorted green print fat quarter:
- Cut 1 strip $3^1/_2$" wide. From this strip, cut 6 squares $3^1/_2$" x $3^1/_2$". Cut squares *once* diagonally to make 12 **triangles**.
- Cut 1 strip $3^1/_2$" wide. From this strip, cut 1 square $3^1/_2$" x $3^1/_2$". Cut square *once* diagonally to make 2 **triangles**. From remainder of strip, cut 4 **rectangles** $1^3/_4$" x $4^1/_4$".
- Cut 2 strips $1^3/_4$" wide. From these strips, cut 10 **rectangles** $1^3/_4$" x $4^1/_4$".

(You will use 80 triangles and 80 rectangles and have 4 of each left over.)

From *each* assorted pink print fat quarter:
- Cut 1 strip $3^1/_2$" wide. From this strip, cut 6 squares $3^1/_2$" x $3^1/_2$" Cut squares *once* diagonally to make 12 **triangles**.
- Cut 1 strip $3^1/_2$" wide. From this strip, cut 1 square $3^1/_2$" x $3^1/_2$". Cut square *once* diagonally to make 2 **triangles**. From remainder of strip, cut 4 **rectangles** $1^3/_4$" x $4^1/_4$".
- Cut 2 strips $1^3/_4$" wide. From these strips, cut 10 **rectangles** $1^3/_4$" x $4^1/_4$".

(You will use 80 triangles and 80 rectangles and have 4 of each left over.)

From dark green tone-on-tone fabric:
- Cut 1 **square** 26" x 26".

From cream tone-on-tone fabric:
- Cut 2 *lengthwise* **side borders** 9" x 74".
- Cut 2 *lengthwise* **top/bottom borders** 9" x $63^1/_2$".
- Cut 9 strips $1^3/_4$" wide. From these strips, cut 80 **rectangles** $1^3/_4$" x $4^1/_4$".

From multi-color light print fabric:
- Cut 8 strips $3^1/_2$" wide. From these strips, cut 80 squares $3^1/_2$" x $3^1/_2$" Cut squares *once* diagonally to make 160 **triangles**.

From fabric for binding:
- Cut 8 **binding strips** $2^1/_4$" wide.

CUTTING THE APPLIQUÉS

*Use patterns, page 30, and follow **Making and Using Templates**, page 54, to cut appliqués.*

From *each* assorted green print fat quarter:
- Cut 60 **leaves** for a *total* of 360 leaves. (You will use 352 and have 8 left over.)

From *each* assorted pink print fat quarter:
- Cut 21 **flowers** for a *total* of 126 flowers.

From tan tone-on-tone fabric fat quarter:
- Cut 126 **flower centers**.

MAKING THE BLOCKS

*Follow **Piecing**, page 54, and **Pressing**, page 55, to make quilt top. Use $^1/_4$" seam allowances throughout.*

1. For **Quarter Block**, select 2 **rectangles** and 2 **triangles** from 1 pink or green fabric, 1 cream **rectangle**, and 2 multi-color **triangles**.
2. Sew 2 pink or green **rectangles** and 1 cream **rectangle** together to make **Unit 1**.

Unit 1

3. Sew **Unit 1** and 2 pink or green **triangles** together to make **Unit 2**.

Unit 2

4. Sew **Unit 2** and 2 multi-color **triangles** together to make **Quarter Block**. Trim Quarter Block to $5^3/4$" x $5^3/4$" if necessary.

Pink Quarter Block

5. Repeat Steps 1-4 to make 40 pink Quarter Blocks and 40 green Quarter Blocks.
6. Sew 2 pink **Quarter Blocks** together to make **Unit 3**. Make 20 Unit 3's.

Unit 3 (make 20)

7. Sew 2 **Unit 3's** together to make **Pink Block**. Block should measure 11" x 11" including seam allowances. Make 10 Pink Blocks.

Pink Block (make 10)

8. Sew 2 green **Quarter Blocks** together to make **Unit 4**. Make 20 Unit 4's.

Unit 4 (make 20)

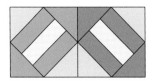

9. Sew 2 **Unit 4's** together to make **Green Block**. Block should measure 11" x 11" including seam allowances. Make 10 Green Blocks.

Green Block (make 10)

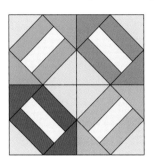

ASSEMBLING THE QUILT TOP

Refer to **Quilt Top Diagram** *to assemble quilt top.*

1. Alternating Pink Blocks and Green Blocks, sew 4 **Blocks** together to make **Row**. Make 5 Rows.
2. Sew **Rows** together to complete quilt top center.
3. Follow **Adding Mitered Borders**, page 57, to add **borders** to quilt top center.

ADDING THE APPLIQUÉS

Follow **Needle-Turn Appliqué**, *page 55, to add appliqués.*

1. Use dark green **square** and follow **Making a Continuous Bias Strip**, page 61, to make approximately $15^{1}/_{2}$ yds of 1" wide **bias strip**. Cut bias strip into 4 **long vines** 75" long and 4 **short vines** 64" long.
2. Matching *wrong* sides, fold **vines** in half lengthwise. Stitch $^{1}/_{4}$" from raw edges. Trim seam allowances to approximately $^{1}/_{16}$". Centering seam allowance on back, press vines flat. Using a $^{1}/_{4}$" bias pressing bar makes pressing faster and easier.
3. Arrange **long vines** on side borders so that they cross at approximately $8^{3}/_{4}$" intervals, forming ovals shapes approximately $4^{1}/_{2}$" wide. In the same manner, arrange **short vines** on top/bottom borders at approximately $8^{3}/_{8}$" intervals. Pin or baste vines in place. Blindstitch, page 64, long edges of vines to borders.
4. Arrange **leaves**, **flowers**, and **flower centers** along vines and appliqué in place.

COMPLETING THE QUILT

1. Follow **Quilting**, page 58, to mark, layer, and quilt as desired. Quilt shown is machine quilted. A circular flower and leaf motif is centered in each block. The border has crosshatch quilting with the quilting lines starting and stopping at the appliqués.
2. Follow **Making a Hanging Sleeve**, page 61, if a hanging sleeve is desired.
3. Use **binding strips** and follow **Making Straight Grain Binding**, page 62, to make binding. Follow **Attaching Binding with Mitered Corners**, page 62, to bind quilt.

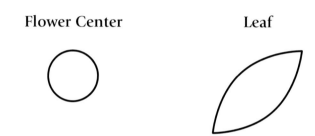

Flower Center   Leaf

Flower

SUMMER CHERRIES

Finished Quilt Size: 69³/₄" x 83¹/₂" (177 cm x 212 cm)
Finished Block Size: 9³/₄" x 9³/₄" (25 cm x 25 cm)

WHAT YOU WILL NEED

Yardage is based on 43"/44" (109 cm/112 cm) wide fabric with a usable width of 40" (102 cm). A layer cake is an assortment of 10" x 10" (25 cm x 25 cm) squares of coordinating fabrics.

- 1 layer cake *or* 30 assorted 10" x 10" (25 cm x 25 cm) print fabric squares for blocks
- 2⁷/₈ yds (2.6 m) of yellow tone-on-tone fabric for block backgrounds
- 1 yd (91 cm) of yellow floral fabric for setting triangles
- 1¹/₂ yds (1.4 m) of green tone-on-tone fabric for blocks, inner border, and stems
- ³/₈ yd (34 cm) of dark green dot fabric for leaves
- ⁵/₈ yd (57 cm) of medium blue tone-on-tone fabric for blocks
- 2¹/₈ yds (1.9 m) of dark blue large print fabric for outer border
- ¹/₄ yd (23 cm) of dark blue tone-on-tone fabric for rings
- ¹/₂ yd (46 cm) of red print #1 fabric for flange and cherries
- ¹/₄ yd (23 cm) of red print #2 fabric for cherries
- 5¹/₈ yds (4.7 m) of fabric for backing
- ⁵/₈ yd (57 cm) of fabric for binding
- 78" x 91" (198 cm x 231 cm) piece of batting
- Template plastic
- Black fine-point permanent felt-tip pen

CUTTING THE PIECES

Follow Rotary Cutting, page 53, to cut fabric. Cut all strips from the selvage-to-selvage width of the fabric unless otherwise indicated. Borders are cut longer than needed and will be trimmed to fit quilt top center. All measurements include $^1/_4$" seam allowances.

From *each* of 20 layer cake squares:
- Cut 3 strips $2^3/_8$" wide. From these strips, cut 12 **medium squares** $2^3/_8$" x $2^3/_8$".

From *each* of 10 layer cake squares:
- Cut 4 strips $1^7/_8$" wide. From these strips, cut 16 **small squares** $1^7/_8$" x $1^7/_8$".

From yellow tone-on-tone fabric:
- Cut 4 strips 12" wide. From these strips, cut 12 **background squares** 12" x 12".
- Cut 15 strips $2^3/_8$" wide. From these strips, cut 240 **medium squares** $2^3/_8$" x $2^3/_8$".
- Cut 4 strips $1^7/_8$" wide. From these strips, cut 80 **small squares** $1^7/_8$" x $1^7/_8$".

From yellow floral fabric:
- Cut 2 strips $15^1/_8$" wide. From these strips, cut 4 squares $15^1/_8$" x $15^1/_8$". Cut squares *twice* diagonally to make 16 **side setting triangles**. (You will use 14 and have 2 left over.)

  From remainder of strips:
  - Cut 2 squares $7^7/_8$" x $7^7/_8$". Cut squares *once* diagonally to make 4 **corner setting triangles**.

From green tone-on-tone fabric:
- Cut 7 **inner border strips** $1^1/_4$" wide.
- Cut 21 strips $1^1/_4$" wide. From these strips, cut 40 **long strips** $1^1/_4$" x $10^1/_4$" and 40 **short strips** $1^1/_4$" x $8^3/_4$".

From medium blue tone-on-tone fabric:
- Cut 5 strips $3^3/_4$" wide. From these strips, cut 48 **large squares** $3^3/_4$" x $3^3/_4$".

From dark blue large print fabric:
- Cut 2 *lengthwise* side outer borders $6^1/_2$" x 75".
- Cut 2 *lengthwise* top/bottom outer borders $6^1/_2$" x $73^1/_4$".

From red print #1 fabric:
- Cut 7 **flange strips** 1" wide.

From fabric for binding:
- Cut 9 **binding strips** $2^1/_4$" wide.

CUTTING THE APPLIQUÉS

Use patterns, page 37, and follow Making and Using Templates, page 54, to cut appliqués.

From red print #1 and red print #2 fabrics:
- Cut a *total* of 144 **cherries**.

From green tone-on-tone fabric:
- Cut 48 **stems**.

From dark green dot fabric:
- Cut 48 **large leaves**.
- Cut 48 **small leaves**.

From dark blue tone-on-tone fabric:
- Cut 12 **rings**.

MAKING THE PIECED BLOCKS

Follow Piecing, page 54, and Pressing, page 55, to make quilt top. Use $^1/_4$" seam allowances throughout.

1. Draw a diagonal line on wrong side of each yellow tone-on-tone **medium square**.
2. For **Pieced Block**, select:
    - 12 **medium squares** cut from 1 layer cake square.
    - 8 **small squares** cut from 1 layer cake square.
    - 12 yellow tone-on-tone **medium squares**.
    - 4 yellow tone-on-tone **small squares**.
    - 2 green tone-on-tone **long strips**.
    - 2 green tone-on-tone **short strips**.
3. Matching right sides, place 1 yellow tone-on-tone **medium square** on top of 1 layer cake **medium square**. Stitch $^1/_4$" from each side of drawn line (**Fig. 1**). Cut along drawn line and press open to make 2 **Triangle-Squares**. Make 24 matching Triangle-Squares. Trim each Triangle-Square to $1^7/_8$" x $1^7/_8$".

Fig. 1

Triangle-Square (make 24)

4. Sew 2 yellow tone-on-tone **small squares** and 4 **Triangle-Squares** together to make **Unit 1**. Make 2 Unit 1's.

Unit 1 (make 2)

5. Sew 2 layer cake **small squares** and 4 **Triangle-Squares** together to make **Unit 2**. Make 2 Unit 2's.

Unit 2 (make 2)

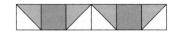

6. Sew 2 layer cake **small squares** and 4 **Triangle-Squares** together to make **Unit 3**. Make 2 Unit 3's.

Unit 3 (make 2)

7. Sew 1 **Unit 1**, 1 **Unit 2**, and 1 **Unit 3** together to make **Unit 4**. Make 2 Unit 4's.

Unit 4 (make 2)

8. Sew 2 **Unit 4's** together to make **Unit 5**. Unit 5 should measure $8^3/_4$" x $8^3/_4$" including seam allowances.

Unit 5

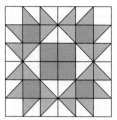

9. Sew 2 green tone-on-tone **short strips** and **Unit 5** together to make **Unit 6**.

Unit 6

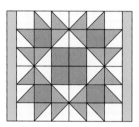

10. Sew 2 green tone-on-tone **long strips** and **Unit 6** together to make **Pieced Block**. Block should measure $10^1/_4$" x $10^1/_4$" including seam allowances.

Pieced Block

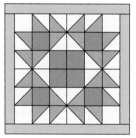

11. Repeat Steps 2-10 to make a *total* of 20 Pieced Blocks.

MAKING THE APPLIQUÉD BLOCKS

*Follow **Needle-Turn Appliqué**, page 55, to add appliqués.*

1. Arrange and pin or baste 1 **ring**, 4 **stems**, 4 **large leaves**, 4 **small leaves**, and 12 **cherries** on 1 **background square**. *Note: The cherry clusters should extend toward the sides of the background square, **not** toward the corners.* Appliqué the pieces in place. Centering design, trim background square to $10^1/_4$" x $10^1/_4$" to make **appliquéd square**. Make 12 appliquéd squares.

Appliquéd Square (make 12)

2. Draw a diagonal line on wrong side of each medium blue tone-on-tone **large square**.
3. With right sides together, place 1 **large square** on 1 corner of 1 **appliquéd square**. Stitch along drawn line and trim $^1/_4$" from stitching (**Fig. 2**); press open (**Fig. 3**).

Fig. 2   **Fig. 3**

4. Repeat to add large squares to remaining corners to make **Appliquéd Block**.

Appliquéd Block

5. Repeat Steps 3-4 to make a ***total*** of 12 Appliquéd Blocks.

ASSEMBLING THE QUILT TOP CENTER

*Refer to **Assembly Diagram** for placement.*

1. Sew **Blocks**, **side setting triangles**, and **corner setting triangles** together into *diagonal* Rows.
2. Sew **Rows** together to complete quilt top center.

Assembly Diagram

ADDING THE BORDERS AND FLANGE

1. Using diagonal seams (**Fig. 4**), sew **inner border strips** together, end to end, to make 1 continuous strip.

Fig. 4

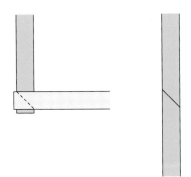

2. Follow **Adding Squared Borders**, page 57, to add **side**, then **top** and **bottom inner borders**.
3. Using diagonal seams, sew **flange strips** together, end to end, to make 1 continuous strip. Matching *wrong* sides and long edges, press continuous strip in half.
4. To determine length of **side flanges**, measure *length* across center of quilt top. Cut 2 side flanges from continuous strip.
5. To determine length of **top/bottom flanges**, measure *width* across center of quilt top. Cut 2 top/bottom flanges from continuous strip.
6. Matching raw edges, baste side and then top and bottom flanges to right side of quilt top $1/8$" from raw edges (**Fig. 5**).

Fig. 5

7. Follow **Adding Squared Borders**, page 57, to add **side**, then **top** and **bottom outer borders**.

COMPLETING THE QUILT

1. Follow **Quilting**, page 58, to mark, layer, and quilt as desired. Quilt shown is machine quilted. Assorted wreath motifs are quilted in the pieced blocks. A flower is quilted in the center of each appliquéd block with a dense looping pattern quilted in the background. The green strips and the inner edge of the inner border are quilted in the ditch. The setting triangles are quilted with a vine pattern, and the outer border is diagonally crosshatch quilted.
2. Follow **Making a Hanging Sleeve**, page 61, if a hanging sleeve is desired.
3. Use **binding strips** and follow **Making Straight Grain Binding**, page 62, to make binding. Follow **Attaching Binding with Mitered Corners**, page 62, to bind quilt.

Quilted by Laurie Vandergriff of Spring Creek Quilting.

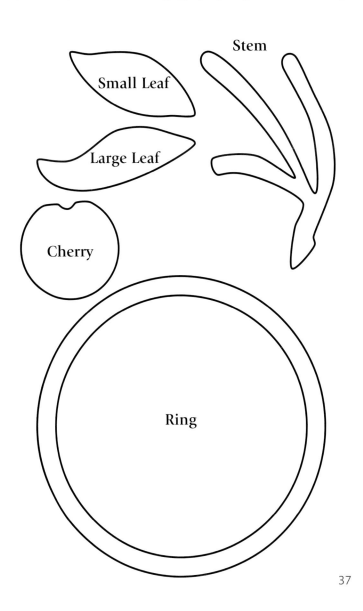

SUNBURST BLOSSOMS

Finished Quilt Size: 65" x 81" (165 cm x 206 cm)
Finished Block Size: Approximately 11³/₈" x 11³/₈"
(29 cm x 29 cm)

WHAT YOU WILL NEED

Yardage is based on 43"/44" (109 cm/112 cm) wide fabric with a usable width of 40" (102 cm).

    1¹/₄ yds (1.1 m) **total** of assorted green print fabrics
    1³/₄ yds (1.6 m) **total** of assorted pink print fabrics
    3¹/₂ yds (3.2 m) of yellow tone-on-tone fabric
    ¹/₈ yd (11 cm) of yellow print fabric
    5 yds (4.6 m) of fabric for backing
    ⁷/₈ yd (80 cm) of fabric for binding
    73" x 89" (185 cm x 226 cm) piece of batting
    Heat resistant template plastic
    Spray starch
    Black fine-point permanent felt-tip pen
    Point turning tool

CUTTING THE PIECES

*Follow **Rotary Cutting**, page 53, to cut fabric. Cut all strips from the selvage-to-selvage width of the fabric. All measurements include ¹/₄" seam allowances. To make templates for petals and large and small blossom centers, place template plastic over patterns, pages 44-45. Trace patterns with permanent pen. Carefully cut patterns out along drawn lines.*

From assorted green print fabrics:
- Cut 240 **squares** 2¹/₂" x 2¹/₂".

From assorted pink print fabrics:
- Cut 100 **squares** 2¹/₂" x 2¹/₂".
- Cut 18 strips 4³/₈" x 20". From these strips, use **petal template** to cut 192 **petals** (**Fig. 1**).

Fig. 1

From yellow tone-on-tone fabric:
- Cut 4 strips 13" wide. From these strips, cut 12 **background squares** 13" x 13".
- Cut 10 strips 2¹/₂" wide. From these strips, cut 160 **squares** 2¹/₂" x 2¹/₂".
- Cut 7 strips 4¹/₈" wide. From these strips, cut 60 squares 4¹/₈" x 4¹/₈". Cut squares *twice* diagonally to make 240 **large triangles**.
- Cut 3 strips 2³/₈" wide. From these strips, cut 40 squares 2³/₈" x 2³/₈". Cut squares *once* diagonally to make 80 **small triangles**.

From yellow print fabric:
- Cut 12 **blossom centers** by placing **large blossom center** template on *wrong* side of fabric and drawing around template with pencil; use scissors to cut along drawn line.

From fabric for binding:
- Cut 11 **binding strips** 2¹/₄" wide.

MAKING THE PIECED BLOCKS

*Follow **Piecing**, page 54, and **Pressing**, page 55, to make quilt top. Use ¹/₄" seam allowances throughout.*

1. Sew 2 **large triangles** and 1 green **square** together to make **Unit 1**. Make 40 Unit 1's.

Unit 1 (make 40)

2. Sew 2 **large triangles**, 2 green **squares**, and 1 yellow **square** together to make **Unit 2**. Make 40 Unit 2's.

Unit 2 (make 40)

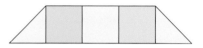

3. Sew 2 **large triangles**, 2 green **squares**, 2 yellow **squares**, and 1 pink **square** together to make **Unit 3**. Make 40 Unit 3's.

Unit 3 (make 40)

4. Sew 2 **small triangles**, 2 green **squares**, 2 yellow **squares**, and 3 pink **squares** together to make **Unit 4**. Make 20 Unit 4's.

Unit 4 (make 20)

5. Referring to **Block Assembly Diagram**, sew 2 **Unit 1's**, 2 **Unit 2's**, 2 **Unit 3's**, 1 **Unit 4**, and 2 **small triangles** together to make **Pieced Block**. Leaving ¹/₄" seam allowance beyond corners of squares, square edges if needed. Make 20 Pieced Blocks.

Block Assembly Diagram

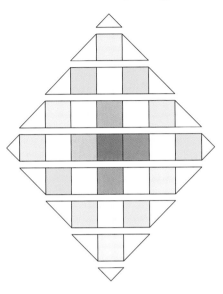

Pieced Block (make 20)

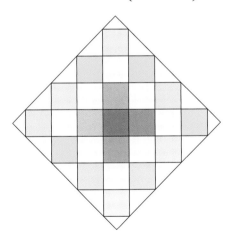

MAKING THE SUNBURST BLOSSOM BLOCKS

1. Matching right sides and long edges, fold 1 **petal** in half. Stitch ¹/₄" from edge as shown in **Fig. 2**; clip corner.

Fig. 2

2. Referring to **Fig. 3**, gently open petal to right side and use point turning tool to form a crisp point. Make sure folded edges are same length; press.

Fig. 3

3. Repeat Steps 1-2 with remaining petals.
4. With right sides together, sew 2 **petals** together along 1 long edge (**Fig. 4**) to make **Unit 5**. Make 96 Unit 5's.

Fig. 4   **Unit 5** (make 96)

5. Sew 2 **Unit 5's** together to make **Unit 6**. Make 48 Unit 6's.

Unit 6 (make 48)

6. Sew 4 **Unit 6's** together to make **Unit 7**. Make 12 Unit 7's.

Unit 7 (make 12)

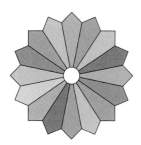

7. Center and pin 1 **Unit 7** on 1 **background square**; blindstitch, page 64, Unit 7 to background to make **Unit 8**. Make 12 Unit 8's.

Unit 8 (make 12)

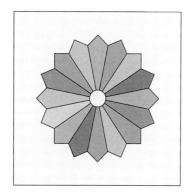

8. Center **small blossom center template** on *wrong* side of 1 **blossom center**. Spray a small amount of spray starch on fabric around template. Press raw edges of blossom center over edge of template, smoothing folded edge as you press (**Fig. 5**). Once fabric is dry, remove template. Repeat with remaining blossom centers.

Fig. 5

9. Blindstitch 1 **blossom center** to 1 Unit 8, covering raw edges to make **Sunburst Blossom Block**. Centering design, trim Sunburst Blossom Block to same measurements of completed Pieced Blocks (approximately $11^7/_8$" x $11^7/_8$"). Make 12 Sunburst Blossom Blocks.

Sunburst Blossom Block (make 12)

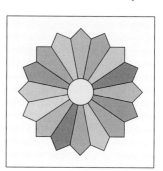

ASSEMBLING THE QUILT TOP

*Refer to **Assembly Diagram** to assemble quilt top.*

1. Sew Blocks together into *diagonal* Rows.
2. Sew **Rows** together to complete quilt top.

Assembly Diagram

COMPLETING THE QUILT

1. Follow **Quilting**, page 58, to mark, layer, and quilt as desired. Quilt shown is machine quilted. A flower pattern is quilted in each Pieced Block. Each blossom is outline quilted approximately $1/16$" from the outer edges, and a floral pattern is quilted in the background of each Sunburst Blossom Block.
2. Stay-stitch $1/4$" from raw edges of quilt top around entire quilt. Trim batting and backing even with quilt top.

3. Using diagonal seams (**Fig. 6**), sew **binding strips** together to make one continuous strip for binding.

Fig. 6

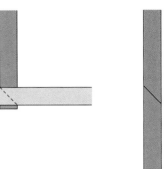

4. Press one end of binding diagonally (**Fig. 7**).

Fig. 7

5. Beginning with pressed end of binding on edge of quilt about 6 inches from outer point, pin binding to right side of quilt to outer point. Mark $1/4$" from outer point of quilt top (**Fig. 8**).

Fig. 8

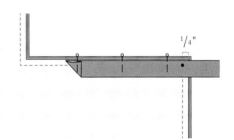

6. Using ¹/₄" seam allowance, sew binding to quilt, backstitching at beginning of binding and at mark (**Fig. 9**). Lift needle out of fabric and clip thread.

Fig. 9

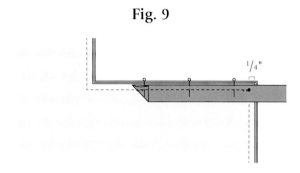

7. Fold binding as shown in **Figs. 10-11**, and pin binding to adjacent edge, matching raw edges. Stitch to about 2" from inside corner. Place needle in the down position; do not clip thread.

Fig. 10   **Fig. 11**

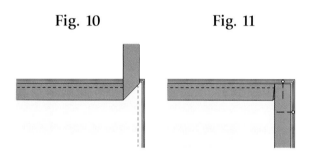

8. Clip up to, but not through, the stay-stitching at the inside corner (**Fig. 12**).

Fig. 12

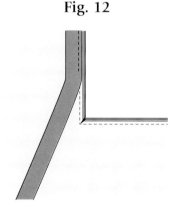

9. Straighten edge of quilt as shown in **Fig. 13**. Quilt top will bunch slightly. Align binding with quilt top edge; continue sewing binding to quilt top.

Fig. 13

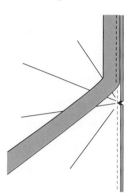

10. Continue sewing binding to quilt until binding overlaps beginning end by approximately 2". Trim excess binding. At inner corners, clip excess or bunching seam allowances of binding, making sure not to cut through seam.

11. Fold binding over to wrong side of quilt and pin. When folding binding at inner corners, fold one edge at a time. It may be helpful to hand stitch folds in place.

12. Blindstitch, page 64, binding to backing, taking care not to stitch through to front of quilt.

Quilted by Laurie Vandergriff of Spring Creek Quilting.

Large Blossom Center

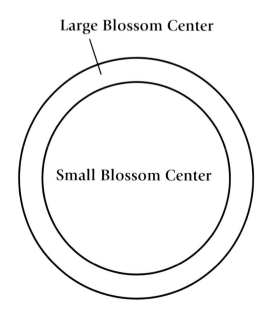

Small Blossom Center

SUNBURST BLOSSOMS WITH BORDER

Finished Quilt Size: 78" x 94 (198 cm x 239 cm)

WHAT YOU WILL NEED

Yardage is based on 43"/44" (109 cm/112 cm) wide fabric with a usable width of 40" (102 cm).

- 1^3/$_8$ yds (1.3 m) of *additional* yellow tone-on-tone fabric for setting triangles (for a *total* of 4^7/$_8$ yds [4.5 m])
- 2^1/$_2$ yds (2.3 m) of fabric for border
- 7^1/$_4$ yds (6.6 m) of fabric for backing *instead of* amount listed for original quilt
- 86" x 102 (218 cm x 259 cm) piece of batting *instead of* amount listed for original quilt

CUTTING THE SETTING TRIANGLES AND BORDERS

*Borders are cut longer than needed and will be trimmed to fit quilt top center. (Refer to **Adding Squared Borders**, page 57, to trim and attach borders to quilt top center.)*

From fabric for setting triangles:

- Cut 2 strips 17^3/$_8$" wide. From these strips, cut 4 squares 17^3/$_8$" x 17^3/$_8$". Cut squares *twice* diagonally to make 16 **side setting triangles**. (You will use 14 and have 2 left over.)
- Cut 1 strip 9" wide. From this strip, cut 2 squares 9" x 9". Cut squares *once* diagonally to make 4 **corner setting triangles**.

From fabric for border:

- Cut 2 *lengthwise* **side borders** 7" x 84^1/$_2$".
- Cut 2 *lengthwise* **top/bottom borders** 7" x 81^1/$_2$".

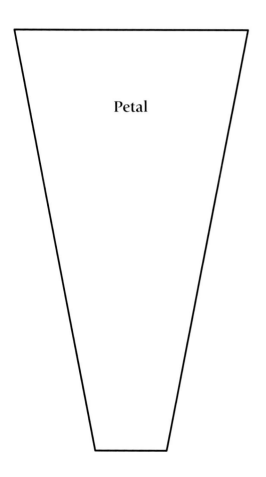

Petal

Quilt Top with Borders

SOLAR ECLIPSE

Finished Throw Quilt Size: 65" x 81" (165 cm x 206 cm)
Finished Block Size: 8" x 8" (20 cm x 20 cm)

WHAT YOU WILL NEED
Yardage is based on 43"/44" (109 cm/112 cm) wide fabric with a usable width of 40" (102 cm).

- 4^1/$_4$ yds (3.9 m) *total* of assorted bright print fabrics (pink, red, orange, and yellow)
- 3^5/$_8$ yds (3.3 m) of black solid fabric
- 5 yds (4.6 m) of fabric for backing
- ^{5}/$_8$ yd (57 cm) of fabric for binding
- 73" x 89" (185 cm x 226 cm) piece of batting
- Marti Michell 4" (10 cm) Drunkard's Path Perfect Patchwork Templates™ and small rotary cutter *or* template plastic and black fine-point permanent felt-tip pen

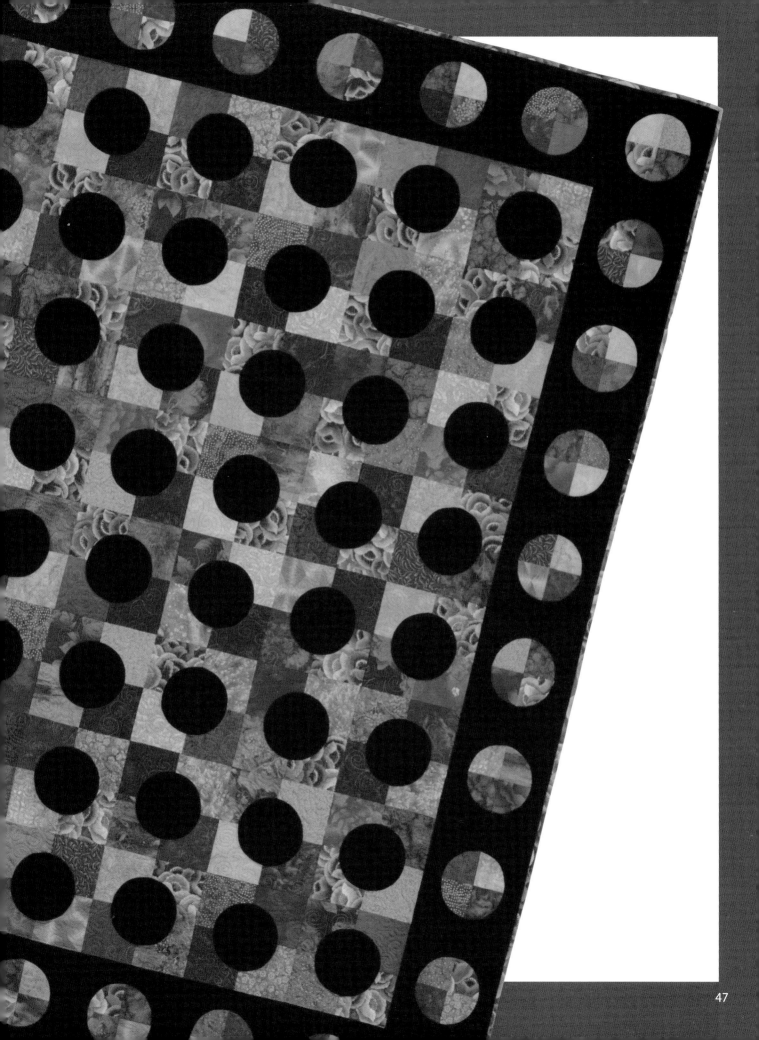

CUTTING THE PIECES

*Follow **Rotary Cutting**, page 53, to cut fabric. Cut all strips from the selvage-to-selvage width of the fabric unless otherwise indicated. All measurements include $^1/_4$" seam allowances.*

From assorted bright print fabrics:
- Cut a *total* of 192 **large squares** $4^1/_2$" x $4^1/_2$".
- Cut a *total* of 128 **small squares** 3" x 3".

From black solid fabric:
- Cut 16 strips $4^1/_2$" wide. From these strips, cut 128 **large squares** $4^1/_2$" x $4^1/_2$".
- Cut 15 strips 3" wide. From these strips, cut 192 **small squares** 3" x 3".

From fabric for binding:
- Cut 8 **binding strips** $2^1/_4$" wide.

CUTTING THE CURVES

To cut curves using Marti Michell templates, place templates on fabric squares and use small rotary cutter to cut along curved edges of templates. Up to 4 squares may be stacked for rotary cutting.

*To cut curves using templates, place template plastic over **Small Curve** and **Large Curve** patterns, page 52. Trace patterns with permanent pen. Carefully cut templates out along drawn lines. Place templates on fabric squares and trace along curved edges of templates with pencil. Use scissors to cut along drawn lines.*

1. Use **small curve template** and **large squares** to cut **backgrounds** (**Fig. 1**). Cut 192 bright backgrounds and 128 black backgrounds.

Fig. 1

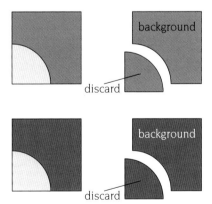

2. Use **large curve template** and **small squares** to cut **quarter-circles** (**Fig. 2**). Cut 128 bright quarter-circles and 192 black quarter-circles.

Fig. 2

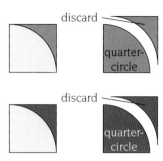

MAKING THE BLOCKS

*Follow **Piecing**, page 54, and **Pressing**, page 55, to make quilt top. Use $^1/_4$" seam allowances throughout.*

1. Fold each background in half diagonally and finger press fold to mark center of curve (**Fig. 3**). Fold background again and finger press fold to mark quarters of curve (**Fig. 4**). In the same manner, fold and finger press center and quarters on curve of each quarter-circle.

Fig. 3

Fig. 4

2. Matching right sides and center marks, pin 1 black **quarter-circle** to 1 bright **background** at center marks. Pin pieces together at corners. Easing as needed, pin pieces together at quarter marks (**Fig. 5**).

Fig. 5

3. With background on top, begin sewing by taking a few stitches and then stopping with needle down. Rotate the pieces and align the raw edges as needed and take a few more stitches. Continue stitching and rotating to sew curved edges together. Keep easing in the fullness of the top fabric as you sew. As you approach the final pin, the fabric will want to pivot out of alignment. Hold it in place with the point of a straight pin as you sew. Check for puckers or tucks. Clip seam allowances as needed and press to make **Unit 1**. Make 192 Unit 1's.

Unit 1 (make 192)

4. In the same manner, use black **backgrounds** and bright **quarter-circles** to make 128 **Unit 2's**.

Unit 2 (make 128)

5. Sew 2 **Unit 1's** together to make **Unit 3**. Make 96 Unit 3's.

Unit 3 (make 96)

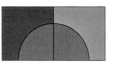

6. Sew 2 **Unit 3's** together to make **Block A**. Make 48 Block A's.

Block A (make 48)

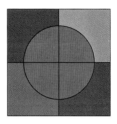

7. Sew 2 **Unit 2's** together to make **Unit 4**. Make 64 Unit 4's.

Unit 4 (make 64)

8. Sew 2 **Unit 4's** together to make **Block B**. Make 32 Block B's.

Block B (make 32)

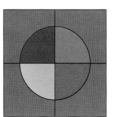

ASSEMBLING THE QUILT TOP

1. Sew 8 **Block B's** together to make **Row A**. Make 2 Row A's.

Row A (make 2)

2. Sew 2 **Block B's** and 6 **Block A's** together to make **Row B**. Make 8 Row B's.

Row B (make 8)

3. Referring to **Quilt Top Diagram**, sew **Rows** together to complete quilt top.

COMPLETING THE QUILT

1. Follow **Quilting**, page 58, to mark, layer, and quilt as desired. Quilt shown is machine quilted. The backgrounds are quilted with an all-over swirling pattern. The circles are not quilted.

2. Follow **Making a Hanging Sleeve**, page 61, if a hanging sleeve is desired.

3. Use **binding strips** and follow **Making Straight Grain Binding**, page 62, to make binding. Follow **Attaching Binding with Mitered Corners**, page 62, to bind quilt.

Quilt Top Diagram

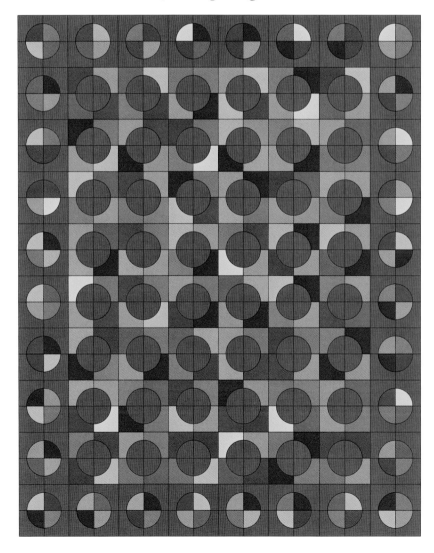

(Continued on page 52.)

	CRIB
Finished Size	41" x 49" (104 cm x 124 cm)
Blocks	12 Block A's and 18 Block B's (5 x 6)
What You Will Need	1³/₈ yds (1.3 m) *total* of assorted bright print fabrics 1⁵/₈ yds (1.5 m) of dark solid or print fabrics 3¹/₄ yds (3 m) of fabric for backing ³/₈ yd (34 cm) of fabric for binding 49" x 57" (124 cm x 145 cm) piece of batting Marti Michell 4" (10 cm) Drunkard's Path Perfect Patchwork Templates™ and small rotary cutter *or* template plastic and black fine-point permanent felt-tip pen
Cut Pieces	48 bright **large squares** 4¹/₂" x 4¹/₂" 72 bright **small squares** 3" x 3" 72 dark **large squares** 4¹/₂" x 4¹/₂" 48 dark **small squares** 3" x 3" 5 **binding strips** 2¹/₄" wide

Crib Size Solar Eclipse

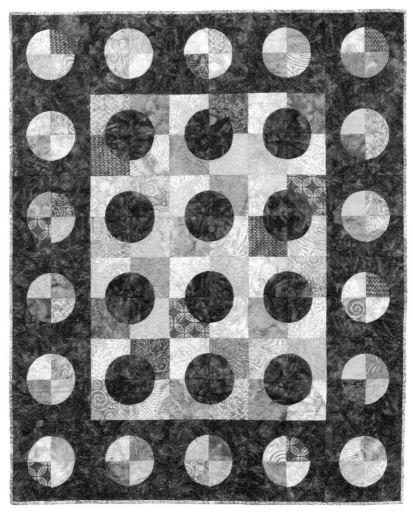

SOLAR ECLIPSE ALTERNATE SIZES
(Continued.)

	TWIN	QUEEN
Finished Size	73" x 97" (185 cm x 246 cm)	97" x 105" (246 cm x 267 cm)
Blocks	70 Block A's and 38 Block B's (9 x 12)	110 Block A's and 46 Block B's (12 x 13)
What You Will Need	6 yds (5.5 m) *total* of assorted bright print fabrics $4^3/_4$ yds (4.3 m) of dark solid or print fabric $6^3/_4$ yds (6.2 m) of fabric for backing $^3/_4$ yd (69 cm) of fabric for binding 81" x 105" (206 cm x 267 cm) piece of batting Marti Michell 4" (10 cm) Drunkard's Path Perfect Patchwork Templates™ and small rotary cutter *or* template plastic and black fine-point permanent felt-tip pen	9 yds (8.2 m) *total* of assorted bright print fabrics $6^3/_8$ yds (5.8 m) of dark solid or print fabric $8^3/_4$ yds (8 m) of fabric for backing $^7/_8$ yd (80 cm) of fabric for binding 105" x 113" (267 cm x 287 cm) piece of batting Marti Michell 4" (10 cm) Drunkard's Path Perfect Patchwork Templates™ and small rotary cutter *or* template plastic and black fine-point permanent felt-tip pen
Cut Pieces	280 bright **large squares** $4^1/_2$" x $4^1/_2$" 152 bright **small squares** 3" x 3" 152 dark **large squares** $4^1/_2$" x $4^1/_2$" 280 dark **small squares** 3" x 3" 10 **binding strips** $2^1/_4$" wide	440 bright **large squares** $4^1/_2$" x $4^1/_2$" 184 bright **small squares** 3" x 3" 184 dark **large squares** $4^1/_2$" x $4^1/_2$" 440 dark **small squares** 3" x 3" 11 **binding strips** $2^1/_4$" wide

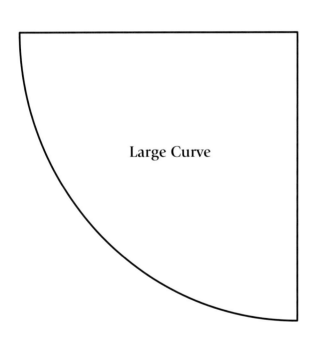

Large Curve

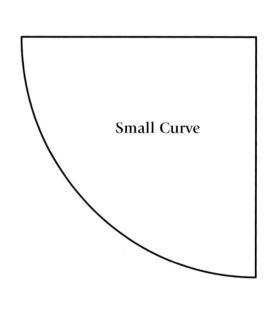

Small Curve

GENERAL INSTRUCTIONS

To make your quilting easier and more enjoyable, we encourage you to carefully read all of the general instructions, study the color photographs, and familiarize yourself with the individual project instructions before beginning a project.

FABRICS
SELECTING FABRICS

Choose high-quality, medium-weight 100% cotton fabrics. All-cotton fabrics hold a crease better, fray less, and are easier to quilt than cotton/polyester blends.

Yardage requirements listed for each project are based on 43"/44" wide fabric with a "usable" width of 40" after shrinkage and trimming selvages. Actual usable width will probably vary slightly from fabric to fabric. Our recommended yardage lengths should be adequate for occasional re-squaring of fabric when many cuts are required.

PREPARING FABRICS

Pre-washing fabrics may cause edges to ravel. As a result, your pre-cut fabric pieces may not be large enough to cut all of the pieces required for your chosen project. Therefore, if you are using any pre-cut fabrics for your project, we do not recommend pre-washing your yardage or pre-cut fabrics. If you are not using pre-cut fabrics, you may wish to pre-wash your fabrics.

Before cutting, prepare fabrics with a steam iron set on cotton and starch or sizing. The starch or sizing will give the fabric a crisp finish. This will make cutting more accurate and may make piecing easier.

ROTARY CUTTING
CUTTING FROM YARDAGE

- Place fabric on work surface with fold closest to you.

- Cut all strips from the selvage-to-selvage width of the fabric unless otherwise indicated in project instructions.

- Square left edge of fabric using rotary cutter and rulers (**Figs. 1-2**).

Fig. 1

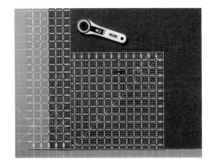

Fig. 2

- To cut each strip required for a project, place ruler over cut edge of fabric, aligning desired marking on ruler with cut edge; make cut (**Fig. 3**).

Fig. 3

- When cutting several strips from a single piece of fabric, it is important to make sure that cuts remain at a perfect right angle to the fold; square fabric as needed.

CUTTING FROM FAT QUARTERS

- Place fabric flat on work surface with lengthwise (short) edge closest to you.

- Cut all strips parallel to the long edge of the fabric in the same manner as cutting from yardage.

- To cut each strip required for a project, place ruler over cut edge of fabric, aligning desired marking on ruler with cut edge; make cut.

MAKING AND USING TEMPLATES

1. To make appliqué templates from patterns, use a black permanent fine-point felt-tip pen to carefully trace each pattern onto template plastic.
2. Cut out template along inner edge of drawn line.
3. Place template on *right* side of appliqué fabric. Lightly draw around template with pencil, leaving at least $1/2$" between shapes. Repeat for number of shapes specified in project instructions.
4. Cut out appliqués approximately $3/16$" outside drawn line for needle-turn appliqué.

PIECING

Precise cutting, followed by accurate piecing, will ensure that all pieces of quilt top fit together well.

- Set sewing machine stitch length for approximately 11 stitches per inch.

- Use neutral-colored general-purpose sewing thread (not quilting thread) in needle and in bobbin.

- An accurate $1/4$" seam allowance is *essential*. Presser feet that are $1/4$" wide are available for most sewing machines.

- When piecing, always place pieces right sides together and match raw edges; pin if necessary.

- Chain piecing saves time and will usually result in more accurate piecing.

- Trim away points of seam allowances that extend beyond edges of sewn pieces.

SEWING STRIP SETS

When there are several strips to assemble into a strip set, first sew strips together into pairs, then sew pairs together to form strip set. To help avoid distortion, sew seams in opposite directions (**Fig. 4**).

Fig. 4

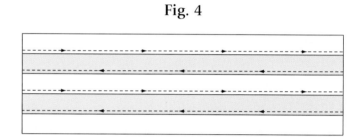

SEWING ACROSS SEAM INTERSECTIONS

When sewing across intersection of two seams, place pieces right sides together and match seams exactly, making sure seam allowances are pressed in opposite directions (**Fig. 5**).

Fig. 5

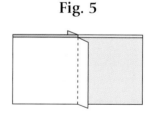

SEWING SHARP POINTS

To ensure sharp points when joining triangular or diagonal pieces, stitch across the center of the "X" (shown in pink) formed on wrong side by previous seams (**Fig. 6**).

Fig. 6

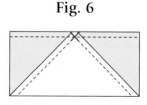

PRESSING

- Use steam iron set on "Cotton" for all pressing.

- Press after sewing each seam.

- Seam allowances are almost always pressed to one side, usually toward darker fabric. However, to reduce bulk it may occasionally be necessary to press seam allowances toward the lighter fabric or even to press them open.

- To prevent dark fabric seam allowance from showing through light fabric, trim darker seam allowance slightly narrower than lighter seam allowance.

- To press long seams, such as those in long strip sets, without curving or other distortion, lay strips across width of the ironing board.

- When sewing blocks into rows, seam allowances may be pressed in one direction in odd numbered rows and in the opposite direction in even numbered rows. When sewing rows together, press seam allowances in one direction.

APPLIQUÉ
NEEDLE-TURN APPLIQUÉ

Using needle to turn under seam allowance while blindstitching appliqué to background fabric is called "needle-turn appliqué."

1. Arrange shapes on background fabric and pin or baste in place.
2. Thread a sharps needle with a single strand of general-purpose sewing thread that matches appliqué; knot one end.
3. Begin blindstitching (page 64) on as straight an edge as possible, turning a small section of seam allowance to wrong side with needle, concealing drawn line (**Fig. 7**).

Fig. 7

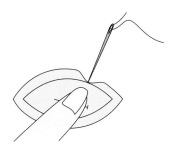

4. To stitch outward points, stitch to $1/2$" from point (**Fig. 8**). Turn seam allowance under at point (**Fig. 9**); then turn remainder of seam allowance between stitching and point. Stitch to point, taking two or three stitches at top of point to secure. Turn under small amount of seam allowance past point and resume stitching.

Fig. 8   **Fig. 9**

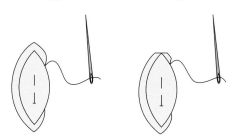

5. To stitch inward point, stitch to $^1/_2$" from point (**Fig. 10**). Clip to but not through seam allowance at point (**Fig. 11**). Turn seam allowance under between stitching and point. Stitch to point, taking two or three stitches at point to secure. Turn under small amount of seam allowance past point and resume stitching.

Fig. 10   **Fig. 11**

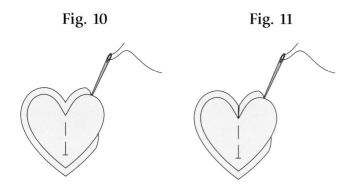

6. Do not turn under or stitch seam allowances that will be covered by other appliqué pieces.
7. To appliqué pressed bias strips, baste strips in place and blindstitch along edges.
8. To reduce bulk, background fabric behind appliqués may be cut away. After stitching appliqués in place, turn block or quilt top over and use sharp scissors or specially designed appliqué scissors to trim away background fabric approximately $^3/_{16}$" from stitching line. Take care not to cut appliqué fabric or stitches.

MACHINE APPLIQUÉ

1. Pin stabilizer, such as paper or any of the commercially available products, on wrong side of background fabric before stitching appliqués in place.
2. Thread sewing machine with general-purpose thread; use general-purpose thread that matches background fabric in bobbin.
3. Set sewing machine for a medium (approximately $^1/_8$") zigzag stitch and a short to medium stitch length. Slightly loosening the top tension may yield a smoother stitch.

4. Begin by stitching two or three stitches in place (drop feed dogs or set stitch length at 0) to anchor thread. Most of the zigzag stitch should be on the appliqué with the right edge of the stitch falling at the outside edge of the appliqué. Stitch over all edges of appliqué pieces.
5. (*Note:* Dots on **Figs. 12-14** indicate where to leave needle in fabric when pivoting.) For outside corners, stitch just past corner, stopping with needle in background fabric (**Fig. 12**). Raise presser foot. Pivot project, lower presser foot, and stitch adjacent side (**Fig. 13**).

Fig. 12   **Fig. 13**

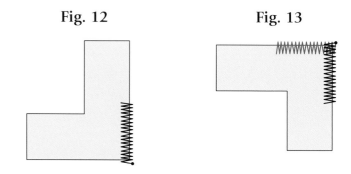

6. When stitching outside curves, stop with needle in background fabric. Raise presser foot and pivot project as needed. Lower presser foot and continue stitching, pivoting as often as necessary to follow curve (**Fig. 14**).

Fig. 14

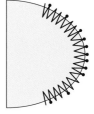

7. Do not backstitch at end of stitching. Pull threads to wrong side of background fabric; knot thread and trim ends.
8. Carefully tear away stabilizer.

BORDERS
ADDING SQUARED BORDERS
1. Mark the center of each edge of quilt top.
2. For the quilts in this book with squared borders, the borders are added to sides, then top and bottom edges of the center section of the quilt top. To determine length of side borders, measure **length** across center of quilt top (**Fig. 15**). Cut 2 side borders the determined length.

Fig. 15

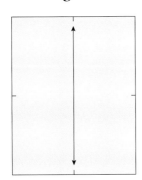

3. Mark center of 1 long edge of 1 side border. Matching center marks and raw edges, pin border to quilt top, easing in any fullness; stitch.
4. Repeat Step 3 to add remaining side border to quilt top.

5. To determine length of top/bottom borders, measure **width** across center of quilt top (including added borders). Cut 2 top/bottom borders the determined length. Repeat Step 3 to add top/bottom borders to quilt top (**Fig. 16**).

Fig. 16

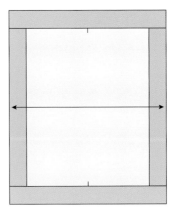

ADDING MITERED BORDERS
1. Mark the center of each edge of quilt top.
2. Mark the center of 1 long edge of 1 side border. Measure **length** across center of quilt top (see **Fig. 15**). Matching center marks and raw edges, pin border to center of quilt top edge. From center of border, measure out ¹/₂ the length of the quilt top in both directions and mark. Match marks on border with corners of quilt top and pin. Pin border to quilt top between center and corners. Sew border to quilt top, beginning and ending seams exactly ¹/₄" from each corner of quilt top and backstitching at beginning and end of stitching (**Fig. 17**).

Fig. 17

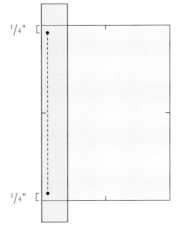

3. Repeat Step 2 to sew remaining **side**, then **top** and **bottom borders** to quilt top. To temporarily move side borders out of the way, fold and pin ends as shown in **Fig. 18**.

Fig. 18

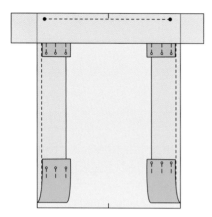

4. Fold 1 corner of quilt top diagonally with right sides together; use rotary cutting ruler to mark stitching line as shown in **Fig. 19**. Pin borders together along drawn line. Sew on drawn line, backstitching at beginning and end of stitching (**Fig. 20**).

Fig. 19

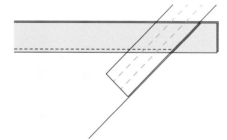

Fig. 20

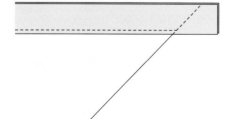

5. Turn mitered corner right side up. Check to see that there is not a gap at the inner end of the seam and that corner does not pucker.
6. Trim seam allowances to $1/4$"; press to 1 side.
7. Repeat Steps 4-6 to miter each remaining corner.

QUILTING

Quilting holds the three layers (top, batting, and backing) of the quilt together and can be done by hand or machine. Because marking, layering, and quilting are interrelated and may be done in different orders depending on circumstances, please read entire **Quilting** *section, pages 58-60, before beginning project.*

TYPES OF QUILTING DESIGNS

In the Ditch Quilting
Quilting along seamlines or along edges of appliquéd pieces is called "in the ditch" quilting. This type of quilting should be done on side **opposite** seam allowance and does not have to be marked.

Outline Quilting
Quilting a consistent distance, usually $1/4$", from seam or appliqué is called "outline" quilting. Outline quilting may be marked, or $1/4$" masking tape may be placed along seamlines for quilting guide. (Do not leave tape on quilt longer than necessary, since it may leave an adhesive residue.)

Motif Quilting
Quilting a design, such as a feathered wreath, is called "motif" quilting. This type of quilting should be marked before basting quilt layers together.

Channel Quilting
Quilting with straight, parallel lines is called "channel" quilting. This type of quilting may be marked or stitched using a guide.

Crosshatch Quilting
Quilting straight lines in a grid pattern is called "crosshatch" quilting. Lines may be stitched parallel to edges of quilt or stitched diagonally. This type of quilting may be marked or stitched using a guide.

Meandering Quilting
Quilting in random curved lines and swirls is called "meandering" quilting. Quilting lines should not cross or touch each other. This type of quilting does not need to be marked.

Stipple Quilting
Meandering quilting that is very closely spaced is called "stipple" quilting. Stippling will flatten the area quilted and is often stitched in background areas to raise appliquéd or pieced designs. This type of quilting does not need to be marked.

MARKING QUILTING LINES
Quilting lines may be marked using fabric marking pencils, chalk markers, or water- or air-soluble pens.

Simple quilting designs may be marked with chalk or chalk pencil after basting. A small area may be marked, then quilted, before moving to next area to be marked. Intricate designs should be marked before basting using a more durable marker.

Caution: Pressing may permanently set some marks. **Test** different markers **on scrap fabric** to find one that marks clearly and can be thoroughly removed.

A wide variety of pre-cut quilting stencils, as well as entire books of quilting patterns, are available. Using a stencil makes it easier to mark intricate or repetitive designs.

To make a stencil from a pattern, center template plastic over pattern and use a permanent marker to trace pattern onto plastic. Use a craft knife with single or double blade to cut channels along traced lines (**Fig. 21**).

Fig. 21

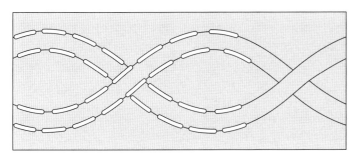

PREPARING THE BACKING
To allow for slight shifting of quilt top during quilting, backing should be approximately 4" larger on all sides (2" for table runner). Yardage requirements listed for quilt backings are calculated for 43"/44" wide fabric. Using 90" wide or 108" wide fabric for the backing of a bed-sized quilt may eliminate piecing. To piece a backing using 43"/44" wide fabric, use the following instructions.

1. Measure length and width of quilt top; add 8" (4") to each measurement.
2. If determined width is 79" or less, cut backing fabric into two lengths slightly longer than determined *length* measurement. Trim selvages. Place lengths with right sides facing and sew long edges together, forming a tube (**Fig. 22**). Match seams and press along one fold (**Fig. 23**). Cut along pressed fold to form single piece (**Fig. 24**).

Fig. 22	Fig. 23	Fig. 24

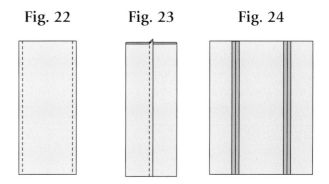

3. If determined width is more than 79", it may require less fabric yardage if the backing is pieced horizontally. Divide determined *length* measurement by 40" to determine how many widths will be needed. Cut required number of widths the determined *width* measurement. Trim selvages. Sew long edges together to form single piece.
4. Trim backing to size determined in Step 1; press seam allowances open.

CHOOSING THE BATTING

The appropriate batting will make quilting easier. For fine hand quilting, choose low-loft batting. All cotton or cotton/polyester blend battings work well for machine quilting because the cotton helps "grip" quilt layers. If quilt is to be tied, a high-loft batting, sometimes called extra-loft or fat batting, may be used to make quilt "fluffy."

Types of batting include cotton, polyester, wool, cotton/polyester blend, cotton/wool blend, and silk.

When selecting batting, refer to package labels for characteristics and care instructions. Cut batting same size as prepared backing.

ASSEMBLING THE QUILT

1. Examine wrong side of quilt top closely; trim any seam allowances and clip any threads that may show through front of the quilt. Press quilt top, being careful not to "set" any marked quilting lines.
2. Place backing *wrong* side up on flat surface. Use masking tape to tape edges of backing to surface. Place batting on top of backing fabric. Smooth batting gently, being careful not to stretch or tear. Center quilt top *right* side up on batting.
3. Use 1" rustproof safety pins to "pin-baste" all layers together, spacing pins approximately 4" apart. Begin at center and work toward outer edges to secure all layers. If possible, place pins away from areas that will be quilted, although pins may be removed as needed when quilting.

MACHINE QUILTING METHODS

Use general-purpose thread in bobbin. Do not use quilting thread. Thread the needle of the machine with general-purpose thread or clear monofilament thread to make quilting blend with quilt top fabrics. Use decorative thread, such as a metallic or contrasting-color general-purpose thread, to make quilting lines stand out more.

Straight-Line Quilting

The term "straight-line" is somewhat deceptive, since curves (especially gentle ones) as well as straight lines can be stitched with this technique.

1. Set stitch length for six to ten stitches per inch and attach walking foot to sewing machine.
2. Determine which section of quilt will have the longest continuous quilting line, oftentimes the area from center top to center bottom. Roll up and secure each edge of quilt to help reduce the bulk, keeping fabrics smooth. Smaller projects may not need to be rolled.
3. Begin stitching on longest quilting line, using very short stitches for the first $1/4$" to "lock" quilting. Stitch across project, using one hand on each side of walking foot to slightly spread fabric and to guide fabric through machine. Lock stitches at end of quilting line.
4. Continue machine quilting, stitching longer quilting lines first to stabilize the quilt before moving on to other areas.

Free-Motion Quilting

Free-motion quilting may be free form or may follow a marked pattern.

1. Attach darning foot to sewing machine and lower or cover feed dogs.
2. Position quilt under darning foot; lower foot. Holding top thread, take a stitch and pull bobbin thread to top of quilt. To "lock" beginning of quilting line, hold top and bobbin threads while making three to five stitches in place.
3. Use one hand on each side of darning foot to slightly spread fabric and to move fabric through the machine. Even stitch length is achieved by using smooth, flowing hand motion and steady machine speed. Slow machine speed and fast hand movement will create long stitches. Fast machine speed and slow hand movement will create short stitches. Move quilt sideways, back and forth, in a circular motion, or in a random motion to create desired designs; do not rotate quilt. Lock stitches at end of each quilting line.

MAKING A HANGING SLEEVE

Attaching a hanging sleeve to back of wall hanging or quilt before the binding is added allows project to be displayed on wall.

1. Measure width of quilt top edge and subtract 1". Cut piece of fabric 7" wide by determined measurement.
2. Press short edges of fabric piece $1/4$" to wrong side; press edges $1/4$" to wrong side again and machine stitch in place.
3. Matching wrong sides, fold piece in half lengthwise to form a tube.
4. Follow project instructions to sew binding to quilt top and to trim backing and batting. Before blindstitching binding to backing, match raw edges and stitch hanging sleeve to center top edge on back of quilt.
5. Finish binding quilt, treating hanging sleeve as part of backing.
6. Blindstitch bottom of hanging sleeve to backing, taking care not to stitch through to front of quilt.
7. Insert dowel or slat into hanging sleeve.

MAKING A CONTINUOUS BIAS STRIP

Bias strips for binding or appliqué can simply be cut and pieced to desired length. However, when a long length of binding is needed, the "continuous" method is quick and accurate.

1. Cut the **square for binding** or **square for vine** called for in project in half diagonally to make two triangles.
2. With right sides together and using $1/4$" seam allowance, sew triangles together (**Fig. 25**); press seam allowances open.

Fig. 25

3. On wrong side of fabric, draw lines the width of the binding or vine as specified in project instructions (**Fig. 26**). Cut off any remaining fabric less than this width.

Fig. 26

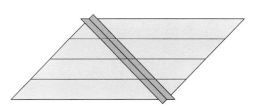

4. With right sides inside, bring short edges together to form a tube; match raw edges so that first drawn line of top section meets second drawn line of bottom section (**Fig. 27**).

Fig. 27

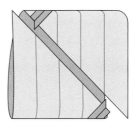

5. Carefully pin edges together by inserting pins through drawn lines at point where drawn lines intersect, making sure pins go through intersections on both sides. Using $1/4$" seam allowance, sew edges together; press seam allowances open.
6. To cut continuous strip, begin cutting along first drawn line (**Fig. 28**). Continue cutting along drawn line around tube.

Fig. 28

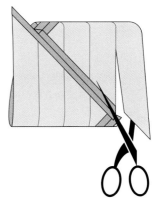

7. Trim ends of bias strip square.

BINDING
MAKING STRAIGHT-GRAIN BINDING

1. Using diagonal seams (**Fig. 29**), sew **strips for binding** called for in project together to make one continuous strip.

Fig. 29

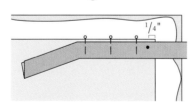

2. Matching wrong sides and raw edges, carefully press continuous strip in half lengthwise to complete binding.

ATTACHING BINDING WITH MITERED CORNERS

1. Beginning with one end near center on bottom edge of quilt, lay binding around quilt to make sure that seams in binding will not end up at a corner. Adjust placement if necessary. Matching raw edges of binding to raw edge of quilt top, pin binding to right side of quilt along one edge.

2. When you reach first corner, mark $^1/_4$" from corner of quilt top (**Fig. 30**).

Fig. 30

3. Beginning approximately 10" from end of binding and using $^1/_4$" seam allowance, sew binding to quilt, backstitching at beginning of stitching and at mark (**Fig. 31**). Lift needle out of fabric and clip thread.

Fig. 31

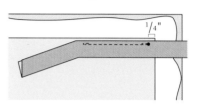

4. Fold binding as shown in **Figs. 32-33** and pin binding to adjacent side, matching raw edges. When you've reached the next corner, mark $^1/_4$" from edge of quilt top.

Fig. 32   **Fig. 33**

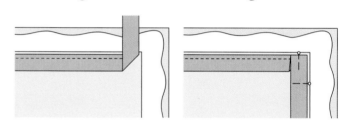

5. Backstitching at edge of quilt top, sew pinned binding to quilt (**Fig. 34**); backstitch at the next mark. Lift needle out of fabric and clip thread.

Fig. 34

6. Continue sewing binding to quilt, stopping approximately 10" from starting point (**Fig. 35**).

Fig. 35

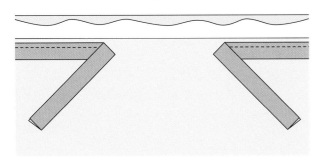

7. Bring beginning and end of binding to center of opening and fold each end back, leaving a $1/4$" space between folds (**Fig. 36**). Finger press folds.

Fig. 36

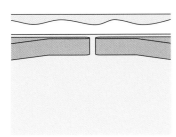

8. Unfold ends of binding and draw a line across wrong side in finger-pressed crease. Draw a line through the lengthwise pressed fold of binding at the same spot to create a cross mark. With edge of ruler at cross mark, line up 45˚ angle marking on ruler with one long side of binding. Draw a diagonal line from edge to edge. Repeat on remaining end, making sure that the two diagonal lines are angled the same way (**Fig. 37**).

Fig. 37

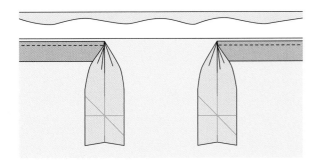

9. Matching right sides and diagonal lines, pin binding ends together at right angles (**Fig. 38**).

Fig. 38

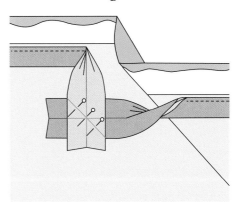

10. Machine stitch along diagonal line (**Fig. 39**), removing pins as you stitch.

Fig. 39

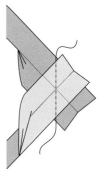

11. Lay binding against quilt to double check that it is correct length.
12. Trim binding ends, leaving $1/4$" seam allowance; press seam open. Stitch binding to quilt.
13. Trim backing and batting even with edges of quilt top.

14. On one edge of quilt, fold binding over to quilt backing and pin pressed edge in place, covering stitching line (**Fig. 40**). On adjacent side, fold binding over, forming a mitered corner (**Fig. 41**). Repeat to pin remainder of binding in place.

Fig. 40 **Fig. 41**

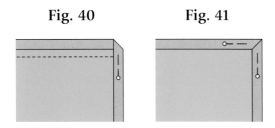

15. Blindstitch binding to backing, taking care not to stitch through to front of quilt.

BLINDSTITCH

Come up at 1, go down at 2, and come up at 3 (**Fig. 42**).

Fig. 42

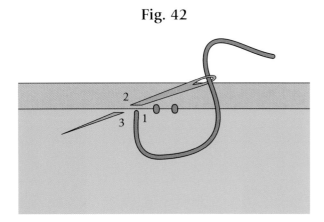

Metric Conversion Chart	
Inches x 2.54 = centimeters (cm)	Yards x .9144 = meters (m)
Inches x 25.4 = millimeters (mm)	Yards x 91.44 = centimeters (cm)
Inches x .0254 = meters (m)	Centimeters x .3937 = inches (")
	Meters x 1.0936 = yards (yd)

Standard Equivalents					
1/8"	3.2 mm	0.32 cm	1/8 yard	11.43 cm	0.11 m
1/4"	6.35 mm	0.635 cm	1/4 yard	22.86 cm	0.23 m
3/8"	9.5 mm	0.95 cm	3/8 yard	34.29 cm	0.34 m
1/2"	12.7 mm	1.27 cm	1/2 yard	45.72 cm	0.46 m
5/8"	15.9 mm	1.59 cm	5/8 yard	57.15 cm	0.57 m
3/4"	19.1 mm	1.91 cm	3/4 yard	68.58 cm	0.69 m
7/8"	22.2 mm	2.22 cm	7/8 yard	80 cm	0.8 m
1"	25.4 mm	2.54 cm	1 yard	91.44 cm	0.91 m

Meet the Designer

Marcia Harmening fell in love with quilting during the long, dark winters when she lived in Anchorage, Alaska. She found that colorful fabric, combined with colorful friendships with fellow quilters, was the perfect solution to the snowy, monochromatic season. As the Alaskan weather permitted, Marcia and husband Mike went camping, fishing, clam digging, and skiing with their three children: Ali, Kenny, and Robin.

In 2010, after 23 years in Alaska, the Harmenings moved to Reno, Nevada. Marcia says, "Now we are soaking in an unbelievable amount of sunshine!"

Marcia enjoys teaching quilt classes and editing quilt books. She began publishing her patterns in 2008, and she is the owner of Happy Stash Quilts. You can see more of Marcia's lively and lovely patterns at HappyStashQuilts.com.